Pressure Under Grace

PRESSURE UNDER GRACE

poems by

William Greenway

Breitenbush Books

Portland, Oregon

Grateful acknowledgment is made to the editors of the following publications, in which some of these poems were first published: *Attention Please* ('Spring Cottage, Mississippi'); *Blue Unicorn* ('In Dürer,' 'X-Ray'); *Cambric Poetry Project II* ('The Day Before the Holiday'); *Ellipsis* ('The Fortune'); *Sleepy Tree I* ('Off Season,' 'A Grace for the First of a Year,' 'Little Pigeon Creek'); *Sleepy Tree II* ('Possum Kicking,' 'The Birth of the Sun'); *Song* ('Prayer'); *Voices International* ('Lake Pontchartrain'); and *Wind* ('Heir Apparent').

Library of Congress Catalog Card #82-1284

Greenway, William, 1947

ISBN 0-932576-11-7 (deluxe)

ISBN 0-932576-10-9 (paperback)

Breitenbush Books are published for James Anderson by Breitenbush Publications, Post Office Box 02137, Portland, Oregon 97202.

Printed in the U.S.A.

Cover art is from an original drawing by Laurie Levich.

Table of Contents

The Fortune, 7

Heir Apparent, 8

The Night Before I Left, 9

My Father's House, 10

The House on the Second Floor, 12

Grand Terre Island, 14

Backwater, 16

The World of the Knowledge of Good and Evil, 17

Little Pigeon Creek, 19

Possum Kicking, 20

Spring Cottage, Mississippi, 22

The Day Before the Holiday, 24

Off Season, 26

Halloween, 28

X-Ray, 29

An Earthquake on American Television, 30

The Gladiator Enters Heaven, 31

In Dürer, 32

A Litter of Kittens, 34

Lake Pontchartrain, 35

Prayer, 36

Letter, 37

The Birth of the Sun, 38

A Grace for the First of a Year, 39

Pressure Under Grace

For Betty

The Fortune

You will go on a long journey:
the land is covered with gray clouds,
the earth, impeccably carpeted
with dead grass.
The friends you leave behind will change
or die,
and letters will grow fewer.
The distant winter trees
will grow in the mist
like gray wool touched with rust.
You will acquire money,
but not enough;
you will acquire fame,
but not enough;
you will have love;
it will be too much
until it is not enough.
You will end alone
far from any light
on a country road.
You will meet a tall, dark stranger.

Heir Apparent

One of my grandfathers was a Georgia
butcher
who beat "niggers" and my mother,
drank moonshine from a paper bag,
and told me
"If you ever squat to pee,
you and me are through."

The other
was a Welsh preacher
with long, delicate fingers
who sang Oh
What a Beautiful Morning
the day his son wed
the Georgia butcher's girl.

They are both here
and they are both dead,
sometimes late at night,
hands on hips on either
side of me,
two giants, each
glaring, defying the other,
while I tremble between.

The Night Before I Left

Scared, my suitcase locked on the bed,
I walked downstairs
to tell him.
Down all three levels I moved
through all the things he'd earned
to find him in the den alone, the lights off,
drinking a diet cola and bourbon,
watching the late movie.
My lips trembling,
I sat down near him and started to speak,
when he leaned up and touched my arm, saying
"This is the good part coming up,
where these natives in New Guinea think . . .
the first time they saw an airplane,
they thought it was God.
They think an airplane is God."
I still see him, bending to the screen,
hair white, his glasses silver globes
crossed by black clouds,
watching natives once again
dig a tiny runway of dirt,
build a tower of sticks,
then sit down on their heels
in the dust to watch the sky and wait
the way their fathers did
and their fathers before them.

My Father's House

Every Sunday, over cheap tar roads,
caving at the shoulders,
snaking through ruined forests,
we went looking for new houses
in the child empty suburbs,
miles on yellow buses
from any school.
The lumber and sawdust yards
were red wounds or craters
filled with sand, bent nails, and half bricks,
needle shaded by thin pines.

Hollow, each house smelled of raw wood,
each room echoed with our voices.
We walked paper aisles across floors dusted
with fine wood talcum.
In the kitchens without water or light,
over sinks full of dead wasps,
we looked at the view:
endless pines full of purple shadow, framed
by unfinished plaster, molding never
quite meeting, and paint
dribbled on the light switches.
We brought our old furniture inside
with us, in our minds,

and pushed it into corners to see
if it would fit,
could look better there.

And when we thought it did,
we bought them and moved in,
brought our clothes, records,
boxes of books and china,
into those houses, already empty,
haunted.

The House on the Second Floor

I see the seasons change
through the window glazed
with white gauze curtains,
which breathe in the long afternoons
of summer, wash the winter tree,
bring flaring red autumn in,
and green spring,
one shade pale.

On this back street
there is no noise; steps
of the occasional old man
going for groceries
are muffled on the mossy walks.
I see him without parting
the curtains, but he cannot see me.

I sit and look down
at their life in a quiet neighborhood
while spirits,
like whispers almost palpable,
move through the high empty rooms,
and glide by mirrors hung

just past the corners of my eyes.

These ghosts I have grown used to,
and they to me; they love the living company,
and I love their awe
as they pass, hushed in wonder at one
not lost into the stillness at the last,
but coming early on—
exploring.

Grand Terre Island

This is one of the last barrier islands.
When it's gone, the waves
will break on the continent itself,
foam in the long sawgrass,
hiss and die. The salt
will wither and burn the marsh to brown.

Millionaires tried to make this
the Riviera of the Gulf,
but there was never any sun, and finally
the hurricanes drove everyone back.
The hotel is still here, weathered gray,
its hundred black eyes staring into the wind
that blows day and night
without taking a breath.
Slate tiles are missing from the roof,
a chessboard without men.
Inside, white lifesavers and
fishnets with cork floats
still hang on the buckling walls;
a plaster crab is stranded
above the door of the dining room.

We walk on the beach among the bones
of fish; the gray waves
seem to be one wave folding

over and over,
carrying the island a grain at a time
back with it.

Our guide tells us you can hear
the ghosts of dancers laughing
and the music of the Charleston
coming from the ballroom above the groan
of the waves,
but I don't even try to listen.
I know no one has died here
yet.

Backwater

There were no more fish in the Gulf
so we went into the back bays
away from the oil rigs
into the green marsh veined
with bayous where the alligators slept,
their old helmets scarred
from the props of boats.
We found a lagoon no man had ever seen
and shut off the motor.
The silence seemed indignant; the sun
stared.

Suddenly, I was afraid and wanted to leave,
but everyone else dived in.
The sleeping rays flew off,
and the crabs, claws up, backed into holes in the mud.
My friends threw beer cans into the brown water,
and stuffed a wadded cigarette package
down the throat of a catfish
before they let it go.

I could feel it choking
in my own throat,
so I turned and watched
the green sawgrass,
the brown roots of it
the tide uncovers when it goes out.

The World of the Knowledge of Good and Evil

I said, you've got to come to Grand Isle.
She said no, the beach is nasty,
there is trash and dead fish
and the water is brown.
Okay, I said, go over to Destin; it's Edenic.
The sand is white and groomed,
the surf is azure, clear,
and you can fish your brains out
and you won't catch a thing
because nothing is there
but white sand and blue water.

Here, there is death—it's a soup,
plankton, shrimp, crabs, all
of this life up for grabs
in the blood-thick, flesh-heavy sea,
fecundity as messy as a birth canal:
shrimp at plankton,
trout at shrimp,
man at trout.

And I have caught them, gutted them,
and thrown the guts in the surf,

and it *is* dirty, as it should be,
because of me.
And when I die I'll burn
and sow the black ashes here
and some tourist will remark
how dirty the water is,
and a fisherman will catch a trout.

It will be delicious,
with clean meat
white as angels
and someone should say grace.

Little Pigeon Creek

What a different need we came for;
they fed on the ideal
we came to find.
We have tried to insinuate
ourselves into this ghost
by flowing with the river, clear
over rocks scoured cold,
where the tourists
cool their beer,
by living up in leaves,
where the bear is fierce
to get what we discard,
and the doe poses,
stepping in a spot of sun.

We came to live in this mountain,
old, with an order once its own,
once with a wild idea
hidden in its shaggy heart.
I leave the broken bottle
in the sand of Little Pigeon,
and the bear teeth of it
jag into the sun.

Possum Kicking

In the evenings we walk home
through stone and deadly golden air
our arms simply full of sacks
which spill in the streets when we unlatch
the doorways, always
hoping on the other side
for rain lips, flower breasts.

Where are the old days
among the old ways
where a young girl on a porch
says goodbye so soundlessly
she loves the evening in her lips.

She is caught just so, in cameo,
her bare feet poised beneath her gown,
her face in chiaroscuro
of thick downfalling hair
like a patch of the moonless mountain night.

She turns and melts into the door
of an old house, wise and white,
who smiles relief in lantern light
for this her daughter, home again.
We would walk our own way home

through the long and fragrant night,
and be there at morning when dark and bright
she runs on the dew like sun and shade.

Which way frosty horses, clover road?
Ask grandfather what he did,
how he lived long nights ago.
Moonshine dance? Honeysuckle snow?
No, says he,
in possum kicking.

Prowl
for the quick two lights,
make a circle tight and close
in and kick
until the squeals
cease to echo in the ideal valleys.

Spring Cottage, Mississippi

The moon is in us and tonight
wakes the old dogs
to one last hunt of what
hides in the darkness the trees begin.

We are looking for a wild man
escaped to the fields.
The whisky in our fists
holds a silver glass of moonlight
as we bend above his prints
webbed like dew along the grass.
We hear his passionate howl
fade into the fat
croaking of frogs.

I slur, "It was the wild man
in you listening,
come out behind you,
howling through you
at the perpetuity of the moon,
staying only briefly
on your dark body,
once his den.

"He's left word in a flurry of quail,
in cuneiform pressed in clay
by deer herded through our sleep,

he will not be back next year.
He has left through the black eyes
of our old gray barns."

"God," he laughs to me,
"if I broke that mirror of pond tonight,
I'd have already paid."
Above a consumptive shade coughing
occasionally near, we both
can almost hear the hounds
of our promise jump the prey,
then follow him away, wagging.

The Day Before the Holiday

Tomorrow is the first
day of holiday
and it's raining
for the first time in years.
The stalks in Iowa
join wet, paper hands
and dance a ring
around Farmer Brown,
standing in his own mud,
crying for happiness,
his upturned face
filling with water.

She is crying too,
about the gray beach,
the tanners scattered,
the aquamarine
sea shadowed
like blotting paper.

I call the national weather
to show her there is sun
somewhere,
but the weather doesn't answer.
All the stations are down.

It must be the rain.

On the beach, the sand
dissolves like ashes,
a blue bucket
fills with water
like a flower dying
of too much sun.

Off Season

> "Yes, these are the dog-days, Fortunatus"

It is the off
season.
The air is pure
mucus.
Women melt on hot corners
like pastel table mints,
trolleys crawl, black eyed,
antennae sparking,
through green, tree
tombs,
and the tourists hide in their motel rooms.

The Gulf is empty.

Husbands wipe sweat
from their eyes and look
at girls in shorts with gooey legs.
The wives just look old.
The courts bulge;
the papers need a page at night
just for the crime reports.

Next door, a radio plays
just a little too loud—

a dentist's drill teasing a nerve.
Then they turn it up,
scanning all the stations
for something called
"fun."

I look at a girl in shorts
and buy a gun.

Halloween

As I walk home the lighted streets,
which wash the jack-o-lantern's laugh,
chainlink fences, moonless trees,
glaring, stark, sheet metal sides
hasped and locked,
and heaps of trash engendering
phantoms twisted, stunted,
hiding human goblins,
warped, wide-smiling, waiting
for the children dressed in dreams,

I say, as I walk home
the yellow evening clubbed
with horns, not haunted with
reeds of the wind
or fancies in the quiet dark,
there is no plasma left,
there is no peace between
shadows of the poles, the rails,
razors, chains, and nails,
no relief between the steel,
here, where everything is real,
where all the ghosts are gone,
though there are still some monsters,
some devils, here and there—
oh dear, my yes, indeed—
devils everywhere.

X-Ray

In the picture you are sleeping,
listening, a little to the side,
toes pointed to one another,
the soft mound between your clothes
striped with summer
strawberry, cocoa, cream.
This is wrapped
in the smoke of my skull,
which questions in the dark
why the bones alone are light
though there you are
between, where nothing is.

An Earthquake
on American Television

A child is uncovered.
Fetal, he is lifted up
and held by a stranger.
A volunteer tenderly
brings him, like a midwife,
from his sudden grave
and holds the dust of the child
in his own.

There were other people in the news
just as fatal,
but no one else unburied
just to be buried again.

The Gladiator Enters Heaven

I thought I was Him for a while.
After all, I won all my fights
and I was loved and strong.
I was ready to barge my way in,
until I saw the real thing,
frail and empty handed,
healing and being still,
and then I knew,
and felt like an oaf, a fool.
It took me a while to recover
after I found out
my big body was useless.
I thought I'd have to change
or die,
but as it turned out
I needed to be as strong
as I was—a bull—
since torture is a terrible thing,
and I was never all that good.

In Dürer

Once,
Dürer won a prize
for his hand
which drew a perfect circle.
Now we have the ring,
horizon of fine line, and leaf, and limb,
and faces like the sun
of every morning
for a year;
a caravan of royalty going round to no place
except to the beauty
of its own grace
in going on delicate camel legs
and swaying wise men
satisfied with their slow
etching on the sky and strong
ritual of color.

Slim fingers
tapered
to a point
of a pen
to a perfect line
which filled
a part of empty spaces
for himself.

Still the circle goes
about a white ghost
who found the bright corona
and made it light the circle
of the shadow he had been.

A Litter of Kittens

Two we gave away, two
live fairly happily in our backyard,
but the other
eats fish with oyster-
pearly flesh, and licks spring
water from a tap on the pier
where, in the early azure morning,
old men in black berets, smoking
briar pipes, clean their catch,
the dark wet boards flecked
with blue scales.

They stroke her with crusty hands
when they leave for their homes
in the inland mountains of a soft pink haze.

Alone, she stretches in the sun all day
and watches the white gulls flying.

Lake Pontchartrain

The wind pulls us through
our cleft of sail;
nearly silent, whisper
and whisper of wave we pass,
all hands laid low
with the disease of sleep,
scattered in cirrus sun,
on a day dying of sleep,
on a water quieter
than the wind alone awake,
and I, the tiller, try to keep
the slot the wind will gallop in.

Sailing, it seems that we may never land,
for it isn't sea and space we sail
but time,
and sleep is wind
and wake is wind, until
the ocean darkens, leaving
I, we, us, our only ship,
no nearer anything but night.

Prayer

Alone, after liquor and late movies,
the ship loosens from the shore
and begins to slide to find
the sea,
to find those left behind,
detached, abandoned, lost
without a word to God.

I set out slightly drunk and heading
back toward the islands of love,
asking not so much that they be saved,
as where.

Letter

After you left that
end of summer
and rowed the lake
the last time,
the land burned
after you;
smoke, snakes curled
at the line,
at the charred cliff
of shore.

I had thought you would go on
forever.

I put the ashes
in an urn
and put it in the sand
and rowed away too.

Now, I go where I do
because where I am
keeps burning,
do what I do
because I find another edge
to burn to.

The Birth of the Sun

> "They shall hunger no more, neither
> thirst anymore; neither shall the sun
> strike upon them, nor any heat."
> *Revelation 7:16*

Forest, dark jade;
clouded morning; melon scent
of mown grass.
The woman stalks, brushing
warm dew onto
her pale, pear breasts;
he is still sleeping,
a forearm over his eyes; he dreams
that when he wakes
the world will be the same, the beasts still
indolent and tame.
While the stones tumble, polish,
into smooth diamonds in the streams,
she finds a blood red ruby
fruit hanging from a tree
of eternal dusk:
a bite, and the sky
cracks and lets strike down
a copperhead of light.

A Grace for the First of a Year

Today was the first,
merest taste, of fall,
like spring water.
Overnight it washed us all
a little.
Now the world is not so much
a mushy fruit;
it has a firmness,
as if you rubbed
a finger on wet glass.
Spring will be like this;
the first warmth will merge
the edges of the trees;
we will shiver to ourselves and see
the stark light yield.
Now, it's hard to believe
that we will ever tire
of winter brilliance,
so precise of resolution
that a blade of grass
and a bare tree
have the same integrity
as if seen twice—
deep in a stereopticon

and frozen in the clearest
cake of ice.

And yet I remember
the smothering early dark,
the sun more like the moon,
the long bars of light
never rising to noon,
a desert of mud,
the land always an aftermath
of some cold flood,
the leaves no longer new
money to walk upon,
our bones empty
for one hot strand
of sun.
Then,
the blood pales;
the trees straighten
like nails.

Yet I can feel it even now,
how it never fails,
the wind, rising from the south,
a wind warm like breath

which has been held.

God of beginnings,
we thank you for your births
which live in the winds,
and thank you that your deaths,
approaching so near,
do not come
to ends.

About the Author

William Greenway is a native of Atlanta, Georgia, where he was born in 1947. Mr. Greenway's poems have appeared in many magazines, among them *Literary Review*, *Blue Unicorn* and *Attention Please*. In 1975 he won an Academy of American Poets prize for his poem "Port Orange Vacation." He is currently a resident of New Orleans where he is a graduate student at Tulane University.

Colophon

The Janson type used in this first edition of *Pressure Under Grace* was set by Irish Setter, in Portland, Oregon. McNaughton & Gunn, Lithographers, of Ann Arbor, Michigan, printed and bound the 1200 paperback copies. Book design is by Scott Walker at Graywolf Press. Fifty signed and numbered copies have been bound by hand into boards by Marsha Hollingsworth, of Port Townsend, Washington.

Library of Congress Cataloging in Publication Data

Greenway, William, 1947-
   Pressure under grace.
   I. Title
PS3557.R3969P7   811'.54   82-1284
ISBN 0-932576-11-7 (deluxe)   AACR2
ISBN 0-932576-10-9 (pbk.)